Disclaimer

No results can be guaranteed

Just to get this out of the way…

In no way can I guarantee any results based on this book and the strategies, theories and experiences in it. You are the only one responsible for your results, I cannot control your actions, therefore I cannot guarantee any results.

Personal results may vary and they are solely dependent on your own efforts.

Let's get started, shall we :-)

My story

Before my online adventure

It was 2009.

I had just graduated from college. I had been learning for sport/gymnastic teacher for 4 years. I loved sports, but didn't really like teaching children. That's what you were meant to do when you graduate from this study; teach on an elementary or high school. So that's what I did. I started working as a teacher.

My girlfriend at the time (now my wife, yay lucky me!) used to make fun of my morning ritual. When the alarm clock went off, I moaned, grunted, yawned and sighed, while taking at least 15 minutes to get from laying down to sitting on the side of the bed.

I hated what I did for a living. I told myself to stop complaining and be grateful. But I still hated it. I never really was the type of person to keep doing something that didn't fit me. Still, I owed it to the school, the kids and myself to give it a real shot. I decided to do the job for at least 6 months and then decide if I still felt the same.

I worked on that high-school for 6 months and one day.

I stood up and left, without looking back. I started working at our local tennis club at minimum wage. I saw it as a temporary solution to have some income for the time being.

I always had this idea that I would do something great and meaningful. I used to dream about earning a lot of money and having freedom to do what I want when I want. Although later this 'dream' evolved into something better, it has always stayed with me.

But as many people in their twenties, I was too busy having fun. I played a lot of world of warcraft (online game), went out for beers often and didn't worry about the future. My dreams went to the back of my head and I kept saying to myself that my time would come.

And so months went by and they turned into years quickly, nothing happened. The job at the tennis club was fine, nice people, not a lot of money but I didn't really care. Soon enough I looked in the mirror and didn't like where I was going.

This needed to change. So I quit this job as well and decided to look for something else. I began looking for jobs in sport, but didn't really knew anything. I've always thought about owning my own business. So I started a personal training business.

I began to train friends and local soccer teams, for free. I liked it. I always had a 'thing' with fitness, training and health. People started asking me for advice and I really liked giving it.

Soon I realized that being a personal trainer needed more than 'just being a trainer'. I had to promote my business and one of my friends suggested I needed a website.

In 2010 I got in contact with The Bootcamp Club, which was a small company from Amsterdam giving outdoor bootcamp workouts. We hit it off and I started a franchise with them; The Bootcamp Club the Hague. I really liked it and over the course of 5 years I went on the build a successful business.

Because this bootcamp adventure is not really important for my story online, I'll spare you the details.

At this time I was also still a personal trainer and I still 'needed' a website.

How was I going to get one…

How I started online

Finding out how to build a website

I needed a website, but knew absolutely nothing about it. I wasn't bad with computers, but also no whizkid. I started researching. I put some simple phrases in google like; 'How to build a website' and 'get a website for my business'.

I used to think it was impossible to build a website yourself. Coding seemed impossible to learn and all those 'framework' websites all looked like crap if you ask me.

After a lot of learning and trial and error I discovered there was a way to build a decent website yourself; Wordpress. I wasn't really happy with Wordpress at first. Since you want your website to look awesome right?

In Wordpress you use 'themes' and it operates on a 'framework'. Back in those days, themes in Wordpress were often rigid. You get what you see. Couldn't really do much with the design, unless you knew how to code.

I decided that this would have to do, although I still didn't believe I could create a website up to my standards. The next couple of months I went to a lot of trouble learning Wordpress and more 'website stuff'. I kept Googling it and I read, listened, watched and learned.

There was something that caught my attention in my research and it was about to change everything...

Key learnings for this chapter

- Wordpress is a solid option for building your own website, but does have a few downsides. Design for me is secondary to business and marketing. When focusing on the most important things, Wordpress is good enough and even better right now. It has greatly improved over the years. I would definitely recommend it over anything else.

How is this valuable today

- Wordpress is still the best option, perhaps even better than in the past. It has greatly improved and for a blog, there is nothing better. It is recommended to find a good (paid) theme though. I use Optimize Press, which is perfect for internet marketers. More about Wordpress later.

A key discovery

So I was looking into all this 'website stuff' and there was something really special that caught my attention.

I ran in to 'the information age'

The information age is probably a term you're familiar with and it was slowly coming to a rise at that time. I had no idea what was happening and I had never heard of it, but it still caught my attention. As I read and learned more about this subject I was in for a surprise. As I went through everything, it suddenly hit me...

People are selling information digitally online

They sometimes called it the 'experts' market. If you know something about a certain topic, you can give advice to others online. You package this in products like ebooks, video's, audio sessions and webinars. The more I researched and learned, the more excited I got. There were already many people like myself, selling their advice online.

I figured that instead of teaching one person in my personal training sessions, I could potentially reach millions with creating content just once. It all made a lot of sense to me.

At that time I got pitched by a dutch internet marketer, called Casper Camps. (He was later accused of setting up people and scamming them, don't know how that turned out for him). But it opened the door for me. He sold me a product where he explained how you could package and sell advice online.

The product did one really good thing for me; it made me believe. Casper showed all sorts of proof and how he did it. It made me believe that anyone could do this. Which was basically the most important thing for me.

I'm not going into detail when it comes to this product. The good thing about it, is the level of excitement and belief it ignited in me. I learned I needed a website, a sales page, a product and I could let the sales roll in!

If only it was that easy...

Key learnings for this chapter

- There was something growing online; the information age. There were actually people making a lot of money selling advice online.
- It made sense that information can be valuable to others, and when you bring value to the marketplace you can charge people for it.

How is this valuable today

- The information age is still growing and operates under that same principle.
- It has never been easier from a technological point of view, to package and sell information online.
- It's a bit harder to stand out from the crowd, that's why tactics to sell information online have evolved and are not the same as 5 years ago. Still many core principles of online marketing remain exactly the same.

My first website

How I got my first website.

I wasn't really convinced I could build a 'decent enough' Wordpress website, so I kept looking for different solutions and I got lucky.

Although luck was about to hit me, you are reading this to learn. Perhaps you want to build a website as well and start an online business. Don't worry, I will refer some very good resources to you, that will help you to do that.

Back to my story.

The boyfriend of one of Suus's teammates from soccer had a business where he build websites. I asked Fred (Iowa's boyfriend) if he could build a Wordpress website for me. He agreed. It was rather basic, but at least it looked nice. That's where everything started.

He build a basic blog for me on this url:

http://www.gewichtkwijt.nl (The time I write this (2016), this link still works.

The website is not used anymore. It could be gone when you read this) Here is how it looked;

It was a dutch blog about weight loss, nutrition and health. As you can see it was in dutch and it was just a simple but decent looking website. Later I replaced this website to erikpenders.com, you can still read the redirection in red there.

Anyway... I was good to go!

The only problem was, I had no idea what to do next...

Blogging

I started writing blog posts. I had knowledge on exercise and nutrition, but no idea what I was doing online. How to create content, how to get traffic, what to do with the blog, etc. So there was no strategy in any of my content creation. I just figured I needed content and people would start to read it if it was good.

I was doing ok with creating content, for about 4-5 weeks. That's where the lack of strategy and know-how started some doubts in my mind about this whole internet thing. I did not really notice any traffic coming in. (At the time I was measuring traffic with the amount of response I got on my posts, which wasn't much) But later I found out that the actual numbers were not that bad.

I had no clue how to measure my traffic. I heard of Google analytics, but when I checked it out I went running for the door. All abracadabra to me. I started to lose faith that anyone would find it interesting or even consider reading my content. I had no clue how to move forward from here. But I kept thinking about that moment I had a few weeks before.

It sparked something in me and I decided I had to be persistent and believe. The opportunity online felt real to me and it was happening right now. So I had to find out what to do next.

I figured I needed to know more about getting traffic and all the other 'internet marketing stuff.' So I started reading books, listening to more audio's and watched more video's. I came across some famous internet marketing 'gurus' like Frank Kern and Matt Carter.

I was intrigued by it all. It made more and more sense to me that creating a business online was possible. But I wasn't ready to buy any products from these 'guru's. I had no personal connection with them. It never felt like they were me or had 'my kind' of troubles. I felt lost in a galaxy of opportunity, with no clue what to do.

So I kept learning from all the free stuff. I left my email with about 20+ internet marketers and they send me all sorts of stuff to learn. Loved that. Now and then I got an offer to buy something and I began to understand what they we're doing. It didn't take me long to understand I could learn from the content itself, but also learn from how they presented the content and how they were trying to sell to me.

I took a lot of notes and one of the first things I implemented on my blog was an 'optin form'. Without capturing leads you could not build a business, was the message I got from the 'gurus'. I put up a very basic optin form on the blog and found an email service provider; 'get response'. (Still exists, but I use Active Campaign nowadays)

The optin form asked for someone's email in return for some free content. The autoresponder was used to contact these people. I wrote emails for my 'auto-responder' with some good content. But never really had anything to sell or even offer my audience. (Which mainly consist of friends and family at that point) More about these emails later.

With all those internet marketers I followed, I ran into a 'small' dutch internet marketer (at least compared to Frank Kern) and I decided to buy his product. It was called 'internet geheimen' (translation; 'internet secrets') It cost me €67,00. I could relate with this dude and it seemed like he had the perfect product for me.

Make your first €500, with a fast 'copy and paste' internet system.

Sounds good right?

Sure I was skeptical, but I had seen the opportunities and I believed this could be possible. With a money back guarantee, I thought I had nothing to lose. So I went for it. (Glad I did)

He had a simple system that blew my mind...

Key learnings for this chapter

- Creating content is always good, but it is recommended to see if people are actually looking for that content and use SEO. I'll show you some tools later.
- Always capture leads on your website, with either social media engagements as a 'like' on Facebook, and/or an optin form.
- Many tries will give zero immediate result and your heart might sink in your shoes a few times. The most important thing is to keep going, no matter what.
- Try to find something to learn in everything you encounter. See what internet marketers are doing, how they talk to you and offer you something. There is so much to learn from that alone.
- You need to know what's happening on your website; measure and track results.

How is this valuable today

- Creating engagement with visitors and capturing leads is still a vital part of any internet business. Engagement is perhaps even more important than it was in the past. With all the choices people have online, you need to stand out from the crowd. Do things differently and always try to engage with your audience.
- Measure results and adjust as you go, if something is not working after a good try, adjust your strategy.

A system that changed everything

The system that blew my mind

The product I bought was a video course that really broke the code for me and showed me a real system, that worked. If I had doubts before, they were about to get crushed...

The system I learned in this course was incredibly easy, but it really worked. I still use this system today, in a slightly different way. These techniques have 'evolved' over-time so to speak. But the basis remains the same. Of course I'll show you both the system I learned and how I use it today. Let's dive in.

Let me get into the basic format this course taught me. Remember that this system is less effective at the time I write this (2016), but it's still used and can still work with a slightly different approach.

The basic format of the course was this: (it's ok if this makes no sense to you right now, I'll explain it all)

"Create a 'mini-website', targeted on one main 'niche-topic'. In other words; target one keyword (something people look for in google). That keyword should have low levels of competition, but enough traffic (1k at least). This keyword also became the url for the website. Than create content about that one 'niche-topic' and related 'sub' topics, that could be turned in to so called 'long-tail keywords'. After that it was only adding some kind of revenue stream to the website."

Some of this might seem Abracadabra to you, let me show you what I mean step by step and give you examples. I will walk you through my first website I create with this system.

Step 1: Find a niche topic, with not too much competition.

What I did: I started thinking about common problems or issues people might have. I started with health related issues. I figured that:

"You create value by solving a problem"

That's where everything begins and it might seem simple, but I live by that rule in my business. Solving problems is the foundation of any business. I used the google keyword tool and just started to type in issues people might have. Like:

- Stomach pain
- Heart disease
- Itch
- Back pain
- Bowel problems
- Fever, flu, sore throat
- Etc.

I tried to look for reasonable search volumes (more than 1000 p/m) and competition that was beatable. So how did I do that?

I used two great internet marketing tools;

1) Google Keyword tool (as I mentioned)
2) Market samurai

Google's keyword tool is used for getting ideas for keywords and niche markets where I could solve problems. The google keyword tool is a free tool that Google provides, that can give you traffic volumes and keywords. It also gives you ideas for related keywords in your niche. You can find the tool here: Google keyword tool

The other tool I used (and still use) is 'market samurai'. This tool will show you (amongst other things) what kind of competition you are facing on certain keywords, which keywords to target and which to avoid. If there is one tool you need when you want to build a business online, it's this one. It can save you loads of time, heartache and troubles. You can find it here: Market Samurai (aff link, thanks for the support)

When I searched for niche markets I ran into 'opgeblazen buik' as a keyword, which is dutch for 'bloated stomach'. At the time I did not know if I could rank for this keyword and related keywords. I had no feel or knowledge about the possibilities and what would work and what would fail.

Because this seemed doable when I used the tools I mentioned above, I went for it. Also because I could create several posts with 'long tail keywords' on this keyword. Which made my chance for ranking higher. Long tail keywords are more defined words and easier to rank on. So for bloated stomach, a long(er) tail keyword could be something like; 'bloated stomach symptoms' and 'bloated stomach treatment'.

Logically there's less search volumes on 'long tails' but also less competition.

Step 2: Build a Wordpress 'mini-website' on one main keyword (niche market)

One of the things that was necessary to improve your ranking was using the keyword you wanted to focus on in your url. (Web address) I locked in the url on the keyword I chose; 'bloated stomach'. In dutch that was: http://www.opgeblazenbuik.net

As you can see I had the keyword in the url. Which is not as important nowadays, because google updated and lowered the relevance of keywords in url's. But it's still beneficial in some way if it's used right.

Note: It was recommended to use .com/.org/.net for your website. Although this is not as important for ranking right now, it's still recommended. These url's look better, more trustworthy and to me it still feels like they rank better. But I haven't tested that.

One of the things I loved about the product I bought, was that it covered everything you needed. So also building the websites. I already learned about Wordpress, but it was nice to get a step by step guide. These were simple websites, so not that hard to create.

Here is what I did exactly when I created the website on this keyword:

- I build a homepage with content of 1000+ words on my main keyword: 'bloated stomach.'
- I created 5 blog posts on this keyword, with different 'long tails'.
- I created internal links to the other posts and the homepage (Note: still very important today for SEO)
- The posts were at least 500 words, but preferably even longer. (1000+)
- I made sure categories and post names used in Wordpress were in the url. Here is a screenshot from Wordpress to show you what I mean. (No problem if you don't know what this is)

Common Settings

○ Plain	http://erikpenders.com/?p=123
○ Day and name	http://erikpenders.com/2016/05/01/sample-post/
○ Month and name	http://erikpenders.com/2016/05/sample-post/
○ Numeric	http://erikpenders.com/archives/123
○ Post name	http://erikpenders.com/sample-post/
● Custom Structure	http://erikpenders.com /%category%/%postname%/

Step 3: Build high quality backlinks

Before I even started step 3, I saw there was traffic on my website with a Wordpress traffic plugin. (I still didn't understand google analytics) The traffic was growing day by day. Sure it was small, it started with like 1-2 visitors after the first couple of days. But still, I was amazed. 'That was really easy!" I remember saying to myself.

The next step in the system was building backlinks. I went looking for big blogs that were related to this niche and I contacted them. I asked if I could write a guest post for them and if I could link back to my website. Some said no, but I managed to get a yes here and there. It took me quite some effort and didn't like doing this, but I wanted to follow the system.

I also didn't really see the relevance, since I already saw traffic coming in and growing. Still, I did it anyway. I wrote 2 blogposts for big blogs and got a link back to my homepage and one to a specific blogpost.

The results were STUNNING!

Not only did my ranking go up in google on these keywords I also saw a big increase in traffic. To put things in to perspective, it was not like I got thousands of visitors. But for the 15-20 visitors I was getting each day, the results were amazing. One blog posts literally doubled my traffic. Still not massive, but to me it was.

In no time I was getting 40-50 unique visitors a day. WOW

If I hadn't measured my traffic and Google ranking in Market Samurai, I wouldn't have believed that guest blogging was doing anything for me. But it was, big time. A high quality guest blog post did not only send me immediate traffic from the post, but also boosted my Google ranking for the keyword.

Another way I build backlinks, was by going on forums and other blogs and posting some reactions to posts and linking back to my website. This really felt like spamming to me, but I did it anyway. I tried to stay as real and sincere as possible, but it was hard to be objective and post valuable reactions with bloated stomach as the topic. I did this, but not for too long. (Only because I hated it)

It's worth knowing that I researched the whole 'back-linking thing' quite extensively. I tried numerous strategies and ways to get backlinks. There is only one thing that really worked for me. That's posting real, good and engaging reactions that add value to the conversation on forums or blogs.

The same is true for guest-blogging. Only good and original content will work. I tried everything, even buying links. It did not work for me, period. The only way to succeed with this stuff is to be real and do the work. No shortcuts. (Btw buying links will lower your rankings in Google, as they only value quality links from real websites)

Also good to know; guest blogging and linking to your website from high quality 'big' websites still works great. Perhaps it's even one of the most powerful strategies to use. It does however have a bigger impact in these little niche markets, than in bigger markets. This is because of the simple reason that it's harder to rank in bigger markets.

To wrap this system up

This was basically it. These three steps. Easy right? Now of course we weren't making any money yet, but you'll learn in this book; if you have traffic, you can make money. Now let me show you how this made me filthy rich... (Ok, almost rich)

Key learnings for this chapter

- Two tools that no internet business can live without are Google's keyword tool and Market samurai.
- I got traffic by focusing on a less competitive, but minimum 1k search volume keyword.
- Keywords in url's are beneficial to your ranking, but less than in the 'old days'.
- It's recommended to use .com/.net or .org url's.
- Long-tail keyword are less competitive and easier to rank for

- It's important longer tail keywords support your main keyword.
- The more (valuable) content you share in your blog posts, the better. A minimum of 500 words is recommended, but I like a minimum of 1k even better.
- In Wordpress you need to set your permalinks to category-postname in settings. (As displayed in the image)

How this is valuable today

- Every point described above is still relevant, with some extra info to add;
  - Keywords in url's can be beneficial today, but only if you create a quality website on a topic. Creating 5 blogposts with 500 words is not sufficient for most niches now. Especially if the website is English and too many competitors are trying to rank for your keyword. If you want to use this strategy, you need to create more content, engagement via social media and quality backlinks. It's hard to predict what will be sufficient, as it is highly dependable on the competition in the niche.
  - Google does not like small, optimized, focused on one keyword websites anymore. They prefer the so called 'authority' websites, with a lot of content. So again, in order to rank with this system, there is more work involved.
  - Later in this book, I will show you how I use this strategy nowadays and how you can use it as well.

How I made my first $9,99 online

The next challenge; making money

The next step was making money. As I mentioned before, the course I bought was a course to make your first €500 online. This meant there was also a strategy to make money with your 'mini- website'. That strategy in this case was;

Affiliate marketing.

I learned about affiliate marketing for the first time. Promoting other people's products and get paid a commission for them. I also read some things in other areas to use different ways of 'monetizing' your website. Like Google Adsense for instance. (Basically let Google put ads on your website and get paid when people click the ads) This played a role later in my journey. But let me get back to the affiliate marketing stuff first.

When I learned more about affiliate marketing I got more and more excited. In the Netherlands we have our own affiliate platform called; 'Paypro'. (You can find it here). There is also an international one, called Clickbank. Clickbank and Paypro are platforms where you can share your products with other website owners that can sell the product and get paid a commission.

These platforms makes it astoundingly easy to make money with other people's products. They create affiliate links for you and all you have to do is use your affiliate link and you can access hundreds of products where you get paid a commission when you sell them. I figured that these affiliate products might work for my website and I gave it a go.

So to put this in perspective. If person A has a product about 'plants' that he wants to sell he can put it one Paypro. Person B that has a website about plants can find the product. Copy his personal affiliate link to this product and put the link on his website. When visitors click that link, they are send to the product of person A, but with a 'tracking cookie' that this visitor came from person B. When the visitor buys the product, person B get's paid a commission for the sale.

Great right? Probably not the best explanation, but you get the idea. I used to think I needed all sorts of 'shop software' for my website, where customers use carts and have a good checkout procedure with many payment options. It turned out for newbies like me, there were way better solutions. Paypro and Clickbank were not only affiliate marketing platforms, they also took care of the entire sale process. Freaking great.

They charge a fee when you make a sale, but only to the product owner. I think the fee was like 1 euro, +8,5% of the sale value. But as an affiliate, you paid NO FEE whatsoever. Which is just awesome. So it was just a matter of creating an account on Paypro, looking for a product that fit my website, copy my affiliate link and put it on my website...

I was beginning to wonder if it could really be this easy. Was this going to work?

Could I just put the link on my new mini-website and let it happen...

Key learnings for this chapter

- Affiliate marketing is an easy and great way to promote and sell products online. While earning very lucrative commissions.
- You don't have to create a product yourself, which is often experienced as hard and time consuming. (Especially when you start)
- Using an 'affiliate marketing platform' like Paypro or Clickbank is safe, fast and easy when you want to sell products online.
- You don't need any shopping cart software when you use an affiliate platform.

How this is valuable today

- Affiliate marketing is still very much alive and one of the easiest and best ways to make money fast.
- Clickbank is the place to be and they have a lot of resources nowadays to learn all the tricks of the trade.

My first sale ever

So I had my website opgeblazenbuik.net ready and already generated some traffic on it. I went looking for a product that fitted the niche market I was in. That was pretty hard, because no one really made a product that solved the problem of a 'bloated stomach'. But I ran in to a product that I thought could work.

It was an ebook called '50 green smoothie recipes'. The price of the product was €19,99 and the commission was 50%. So €9,00 whenever you make a sale. I got my affiliate link for the product and I put the link inside a banner of the product. I put it on my website and waited.

Of course this product wasn't a great 'market fit' as we call it. But it made a little bit of sense, since green smoothies can help with obstipation and a bloated stomach.

I was expecting nothing really, because it just felt too easy. I was probably missing something, I thought. I checked my account about 40 times a day to see if anything had happened. Nothing after one day…

I could track (inside Paypro) if people actually visited the page with my affiliate link on it and they were. I could also track if people clicked the link and went to the sales page of the product, the answer was yes. (Not a lot, but a few clicks in the first days did not seem bad to me)

After just two days it happened… My very first sale ever made online. I was almost dancing on the table. OMG!

Here is the screenshot from Paypro, you can see the time and the date I made my very first €9,00 ever. I don't use Paypro anymore, because later in my journey I started processing sales myself. All the affiliate work I do right now, are on international platforms like Clickbank, which works the same but International.

The white field (with the awesome smiley) contains some details underneath I want to share in the next chapter with you. That's why I put the white field there.

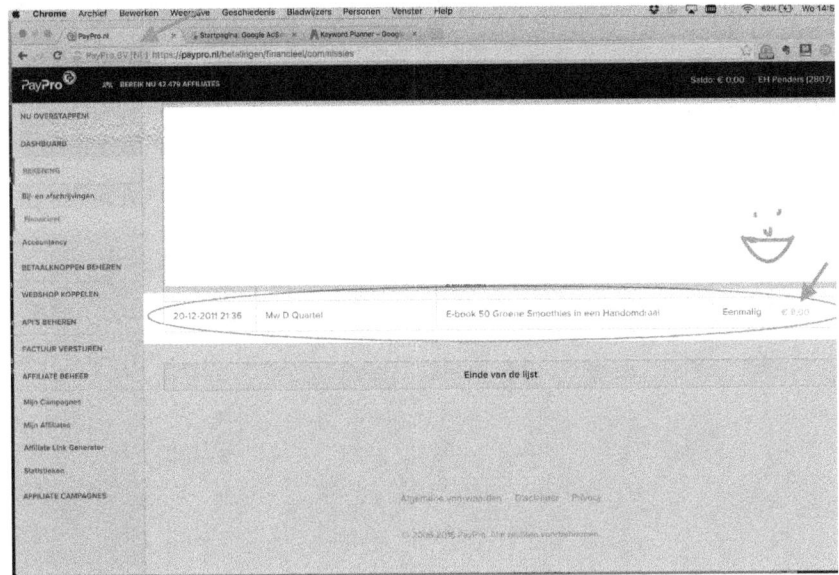

I was just flabbergasted to say the least. This was too easy..... I couldn't really believe it... how can something this easy, already generate results? You can imagine that this got me very excited.

I figured that the process I used can be repeated as much times as I'd like. I began to dream of the possibilities and I couldn't wait to get moving. So that's exactly what I did.

Key learnings for this chapter

- An affiliate product does not have to be a 'perfect marketing fit', although the better it fits, the higher your conversions. (People that actually buy from you, versus the visitors on your website)

How this is valuable today

- 'Market fit' becomes more and more important when it comes to affiliate marketing. The main reason for that might be the skepticism of consumers when it comes to digital products. As the market is flooded the last couple of years, people seem to be a little bit more hesitant with buying. Perhaps they get pitched and sold to so much right now, market fit plays an important role. For instance, when you have a blog with your main keyword being 'bloated stomach', you are much better off selling a problem solver like a supplement that relieves bloated stomach symptoms than an ebook with green smoothies. (NOTE: This doesn't mean it's necessarily harder to stand out from the crowd. If you provide some real value, you actually stand out from the crowd faster than 5 years ago.)

How I went from $9,99 to more than $100

Repeating the system

After I put affiliate links to the smoothie ebook all over opgeblazenbuik.net, I created three more mini websites back to back. One was 'koolhydraatarmbrood.net' (translated: 'lowcarb-bread'), the second was 'koolhydraatarmeproducten.net' (translated: 'lowcarb-products') and the third was: 'conditieopbouwen.org' (translated: 'building condition')

Although I couldn't solve a problem directly with the first two keywords and therefore didn't have a good market-fit affiliate-product for it, I did see an opportunity when I ran into these keywords. The competition was so low, that I knew from my experience with the first blog, that I could rank on these keywords even faster. (At least that was my conviction)

Besides that, I figured that most people looking for 'low-carb' are somehow interested in dieting or losing weight. Perhaps not the perfect market-fit, but I decided to give it a go.

'Conditieobouwen.org' had a lower search volume and was a bit harder to rank for, but since I was personally into this stuff, I figured it was easier to create more and better content.

I did the same thing with these three 'mini-blogs' as I did with the first one. So I went through the entire system again and build them from scratch. I won't go in to detail on these websites, because I did the exact same thing. Building these websites went quite fast once you I got the hang of it.

After they were done, I almost instantly got traffic going on these websites. (The most on koolhydraatarmbrood.net, because the average search volume was a lot higher and the competition was slightly lower than the other ones.)

I added affiliate links on the 'low carb' websites, with one of the best selling products on Paypro, a diet called 'het mentale dieetplan'. Which translates to 'the mental diet'. On conditieopbouwen.org I put a training program with kettle bells.

Just like that, wham bam done.

These three mini website were done within 10 days, and I didn't work my tail off. Traffic volume was growing and I saw no reason why this wouldn't work.

And I was right...

Key learnings for this chapter

- When you see an opportunity that does not meet certain 'requirements', look at how strong the benefits of this opportunity are. Sometimes you go for something, despite having some odds against you. If you are confident it will work, it most often does. Building a business online is never one straight line up. Try, adjust and keep trying.
- Once you find out a system that works, copy and paste and leverage good results.

What happened next...

The websites were done, the affiliate links were placed inside banners or images and I waited. As it turned out, I didn't have to wait long...

I was pretty lazy the coming days, I was only checking Paypro like 400 times a day. I understand why I did it, because it's tempting. But in hindsight it wasn't the best thing to do, because the moment you stop working you fall behind.

Not literally, but the key to this kind of business for me is to keep going no matter what. I've said it before and you'll probably hear it a few times more. Anyway, so I was checking Paypro too much and it didn't take long before the first result came in.

Here is the screenshot of what happened:

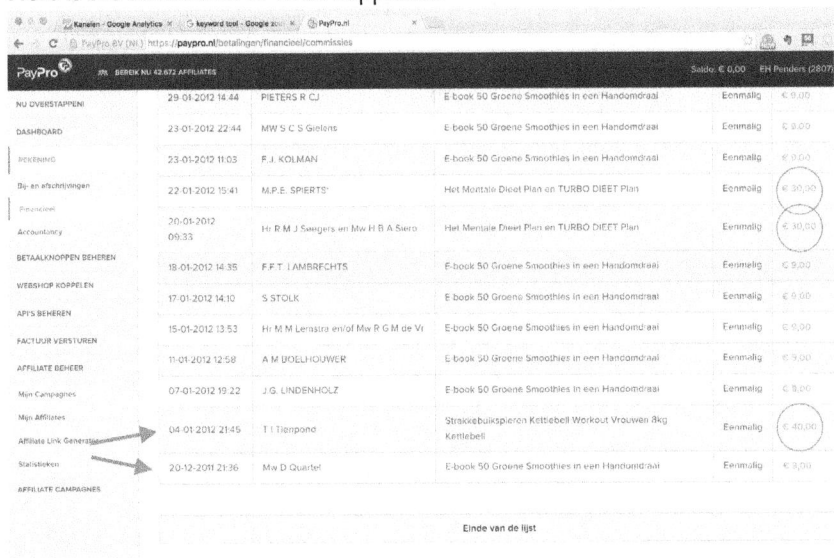

I almost fell of my chair, literally. OMG!

This was amazing. Within 15 days of my first sale ever, I made $40,00 instantly from the kettlebell product on conditieopbouwen.org. The smoothie ebook kept selling as you can see and 2,5 weeks later I sold the diet product on the 'low carb' mini websites. I made a whopping $30,00 on these sales. And it was just SO easy.

I made more than $100 after a couple of weeks and it all felt super easy.

This might not seem like a lot of money and the sales did not fly in one by one, but it proved this system worked and I just loved the fact that you could make money while sleeping or hanging out with your friends. (To me that's one of the best feelings in the world) Also note that it did not take a lot of time or effort to create. At least it did not feel like a lot of work.

All this time I was also running a bootcamp business, which was a full time job...

After doing this, I created some more mini-websites which I will not be covering in detail. Some did good, others didn't do so good. But something else came up in my mind. (As it always does) The question: 'Ok what's next', is as great as it is annoying. I started thinking about those affiliates and I asked myself this;

"Could I create my own product and see if anyone else is willing to sell it for a commission?"

From my own experience I knew there had to be more people looking for products to sell and looking for ways to make money online. Perhaps there we're people that already had a good website with lots of traffic, but no way to monetize that.

It turned out, I was right, again... (Never underestimate common sense and your gut telling you stuff ;-))

Key learnings for this chapter

- It's very easy to get distracted. Especially if you're anything like me. If you have a strong reason to keep going, you'll probably will. Do understand that the fire of enthusiasm will always disappear somewhere in the process. That's when your success is either build or torn down. Keep going, no matter what.
- 'What's next' is a fine question that will challenge you. But never devalue what you've done, achieved and where you come from. It's worth a lot.

How I went from $100-$500

My own product

In the meanwhile my mini-websites were generating sales, I wanted to create a product myself. I pondered what to create for a while, but I came up with an ebook quite fast. It felt 'not impossible' to create. I was pretty confident I could at least create content with my knowledge on the topic. Even though I had never written one word in my life.

I decided to go for it and I started writing.

I created an ebook called; 'Hardlopend afslanken'. Which translates to something like; 'Lose weight with running'. It took me a few days to write a first draft of this book. Never expected that. I thought it would take me months. I created a simple cover myself. Here's how it looked;

Not a real beauty, but it was good enough. I think I created this cover with Boxshot 3d at the time. If you want a good place to create a free cover now, I would recommend myecovermaker.com (Create an account, some formats are free) But I'm drifting off topic here, back to the story.

After the first draft, I started revising and editing. That took a while, as I had dumped all my thoughts on paper. But it worked and I was done within 2,5 weeks. Writing a book can be challenging, but there are some good ways to do it. Especially if you write about a topic you know a lot about.

I like to create a fast general outline with a brainstorm session and then dump everything in my head on paper. To me it's easier to edit later and add or remove certain pieces than to start 'organized', if you know what I mean. I like to put every little brainfart on paper and often I have to do a lot of editing, which is fine.

The next thing I needed was a place to sell this bad boy. If other people (affiliates) were also going to sell this (that was the goal) than I needed a sales page. Which is one single page, with the sole purpose of selling. So affiliates could send traffic to that specific page, that was designed to sell the book.

No distractions, just good copy, a good offer and a call to action. I just found out this website is still online, you can find it here. Back in those days (2011/2012), these kind of sales pages worked incredibly well. Nowadays they are less effective. People are more skeptical and I believe these kind of pages raise suspicion with people. But these things can and should be tested when you use them. Here's a screenshot of the page;

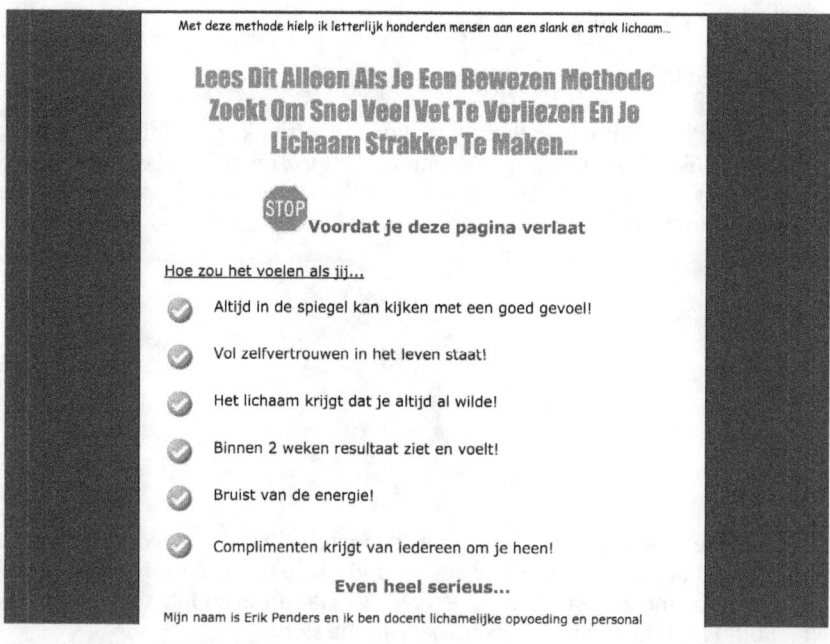

The page is in dutch (sorry for that) and it's modeled after AIDA. Google Aida if you want to check it out. Although these pages might be less effective now, I believe AIDA still works very well but in a slightly different way. Cleaner and more trustworthy pages, no more red headlines and you might be able to pull off a very good sales page today.

Affiliates for the book were asked to send their visitors to this page. Paypro handled the transaction and tracked where the traffic came from for the commissions.

The challenge now was selling the book. Selling it myself, but also finding affiliates. The first question was easily answered it turned out.

Because I had forgotten something, that came in very handy...

Key learnings for this chapter

- Writing is not as hard as it might seem. If you want to learn, you'll get better over time. I still don't really consider myself a writer, as I'm on the shoulders of giants. But I write despite all the flaws and crap I put on paper. I write because I want to contribute and there no reason why you couldn't contribute as well. (If you want to)
- If you want to write a book I would recommend creating a 'general outline' of the story and then dumping all your thought on every topic on paper. Edit later.
- A sales page is a single page with the sole purpose of selling. These pages are crucial in selling products online and should never be forgotten in an internet business.
- Aida is still a good model that works for sales pages.

Previous work paid off

Meanwhile I hadn't been paying too much attention to my blog. Remember gewichtkwijt.nl? Fred build it for me and I wrote a bunch of blog posts, but I didn't do any work on it when I went through the course and started to create those 'mini-websites'.

But it popped back in my head when I was thinking about selling the ebook. Gewichtkwijt translates to 'lose weight' and it was the perfect fit for my ebook. So I went over to take a look a look. By that time I had 'sort of' figured out Google analytics and I fired it up to check out the traffic.

I was kinda hoping it wasn't too bad after neglecting this blog for weeks...

When I opened Google analytics I was amazed. Traffic had been increasing almost every single day. Just from a bunch of blogposts. I had done nothing with SEO, as I had no knowledge on SEO when I was writing the blog posts.

Again I had a moment of; "omg! This can't be this easy!" But it was. I have to say that it's not this easy anymore. It's almost impossible to get traffic without doing proper SEO. This is especially true when your website is English, as there are much more websites trying to rank.

With gewichtkwijt.nl I was a bit lucky to have used some low competition dutch keywords in my titles and posts, that did have a few hundred in search volume each month. Let's say I wasn't unhappy with it, because now I had another platform for selling my ebook.

I also told you earlier that I put an optin form on this website, to capture leads. (Also totally forgotten about that) I took a look in my getresponse account to see if I had any signups... There were 70 people on my list, that later did not seem very useful. It gave me only one sale. Still I was happy that I build a list of 70 people, again with no serious effort.

I put the link to my sales page on gewichtkwijt.nl and also added it to some blog posts. This made some sales for me every once in a while, not a lot. (I'll show you in a second)

But there was something better about to happen...

Key learnings for this chapter

- Blogposts will continue to create free traffic for you long after you've posted them. Especially if you optimized your post and put some

awesome and valuable content in there.
- Never forget an optin form on your website, it's vital to your business

The power of affiliates

As you will see in a little while, getting affiliates was one of the best moves I made. These affiliates can be found on affiliate platforms, but also just by googling for certain niche websites.

I checked out all the companies/websites with products on Paypro, but never really found any good fits. I tried to contact some here and there, but got nothing out of it. The main reason for this was the size of Paypro. At the time there just weren't enough product owners and businesses selling on Paypro.

I had to think of something else, so that's what I did…

The book was about losing weight with running and I asked myself who or what kind of website might be interested in this type of book. The answer was simple, it had to be either websites about weight loss or about running.

I know we had some big running websites in the Netherlands, so I started looking. I came across several, which I all contacted. One of the websites was about to become an affiliate for my ebook, just by sending a few emails. The website that replied to me with interest was; http://www.hardlopen.nl (translates to www.running.nl)

Which was one of the biggest running websites in the Netherlands. The website owner had a lot of traffic, but never really learned how to monetize his website. There I was, explaining this whole affiliate thing to him.

He never really hesitated and he started affiliating for my ebook. That's when it really took off. (Well for a rookie beginner it did).. So here's what happened. Especially notice the dates where these sales took place. All the little 5,57 sales were from my affiliate, which was all just because I contacted him and he put my book on this website… Amazing right?

You can see a few 14,07 sales, which was my ebook directly from my own blog. Also not bad. And the products I affiliated for kept selling once every few days.

This was absolutely amazing to me.

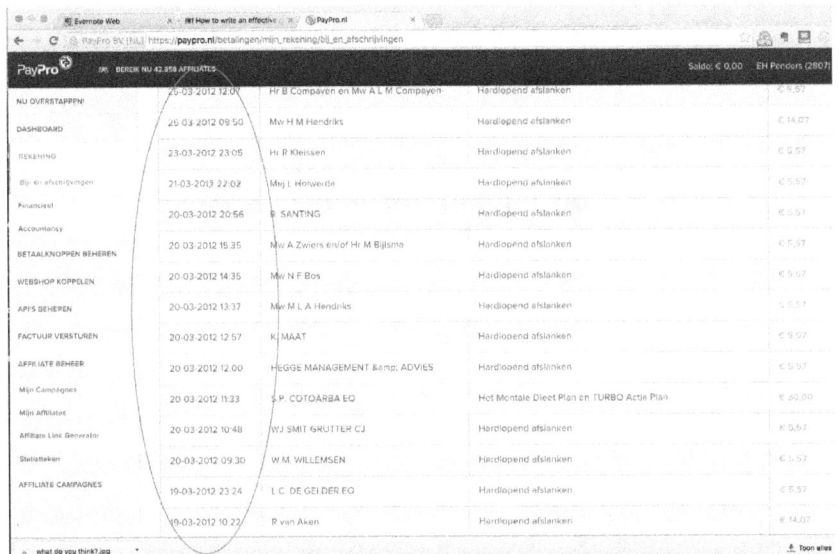

I had this great system in place that I had proved to myself worked. Now it wasn't all roses and sunshine. I ran in to some troubles later and sales went down. But I did have a proven system in my hands here, that was quite easy to build. I started thinking about growing this business. The next step I figured would either be; building more mini-websites or, focus more on affiliates, my main blog and my ebook.

Looking back on it all now, I probably didn't make the best choice at this point...

Key learnings for this chapter

- You can learn all the strategies in the world but they will never beat common sense. Take some time to step back and think about your business. If you want to find affiliates, just simply contacting the right people can go a long way. Remember that you want something from them, not the other way around. Always try to add value for them and see how you can help them out. They will be much more willing to help you, once you've helped them.

How I went from $600 to $1000

Building more mini website

I decided to build more mini-websites. In hindsight the smart thing would have been finding more affiliates for my ebook. The results from the one affiliate with my own ebook, were far better than the results from the mini-websites I build. I was probably a bit scared that people wouldn't like the ebook and the mini-websites weren't as personal.

So if they would fail, it wouldn't really effect me personally. Whereas the ebook felt very personal and it scared me that people could criticize it. (Chicken) So I took the 'easy' way out and starting building more mini websites. I had proven this system worked as well, so I went for it. Before I knew it I had build around 10 more mini websites. And I ran in to some troubles.

Because I was looking for low competition niches, I ran in to traffic that wasn't really looking for a place to spend their money. I mentioned the 'market-fit' phrase before. Websites about skin troubles, lung issues and poems weren't really places to sell products. They probably weren't looking to buy and there was no product that fit these markets.

So it did not go so well...

I hardly sold anything from these websites and I realized I was pulling a dead horse here. (Dutch proverb I think, it means that this wasn't working at all) I was getting ok traffic on all these websites, but hardly to no sales at all. I had to find a different way to monetize the traffic I was generating on these websites.

Because all these mini websites combined had a decent amount of traffic...

Key learnings for this chapter

-   If you know everything up front, building a business is easy. But you don't. Trial and error is a logical process when building a business and it's totally fine to make mistakes. Often mistakes still posses some sort of opportunity.

Other revenue streams

So the question was; 'how could I monetize these websites besides affiliate products?' I had read about people making more than 20k per month with Google Adsense and I looked in to it. Adsense is a platform where website owners can ask google to display ads on their websites.

In return you get paid a commission for clicks on these advertisements. Depending on your market and the ads, these clicks went somewhere from $0,05 to $15,00. Perhaps even more in certain markets. Google places ads that suit your website, or at least they try do so.

This means if your website is about weight loss, Google ads will also be about weight loss. Which makes it a better market-fit than affiliating in this case. Also you did not need to make a sale, only get a click on an advertisement.

The downside is the amount of money it generates, every click is worth far less than selling a product. Still, clicks are easier to get than product sales. I decided to try this for the websites that weren't selling much with affiliate products...

I created a Google Adsense account, which is pretty straight forward and can be easily done by following Google's guidelines. (If you do this, please remember to never click on your own ads) After that it was pretty simple to get ads on the websites, it was a matter of creating an ad block and copying html to your websites. Pretty straightforward and I had all the ads running within a few hours.

Here's a screenshot of what they did the first couple of months;

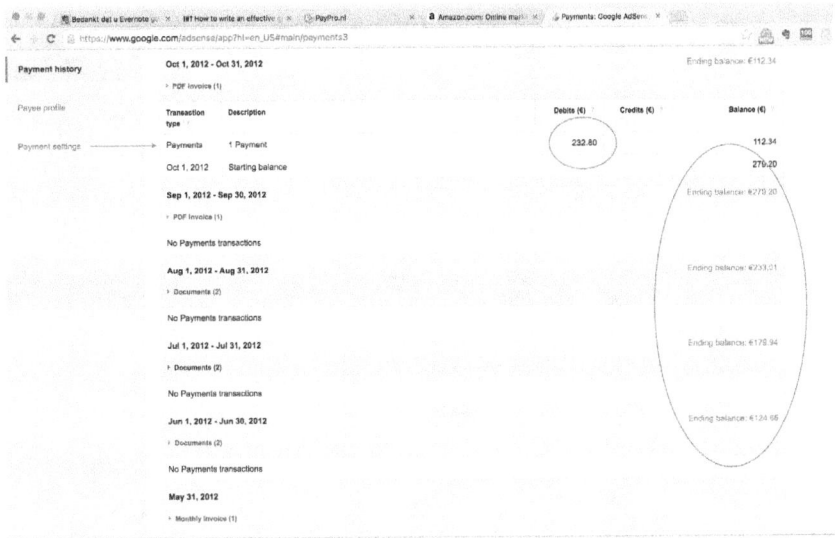

I made about 50,00 a month from these websites. Which again, is not a lot. But it was starting to add up, my affiliate websites, my own ebook and affiliate for it and Google Adsense. Altogether that made me a decent amount of money and I loved it.

Key learnings for this chapter

- Google Adsense is a very easy and lucrative way to monetize a website. But if you want it to make a substantial amount of money, you need loads of traffic. Running into thousands per month at the very least.

The #1 key lesson

I made a few thousand dollars with these strategies. I did that with very limited time. Here's a screenshot from the money I pulled out of Paypro. When I started writing this book, I even found some money left in there lol;

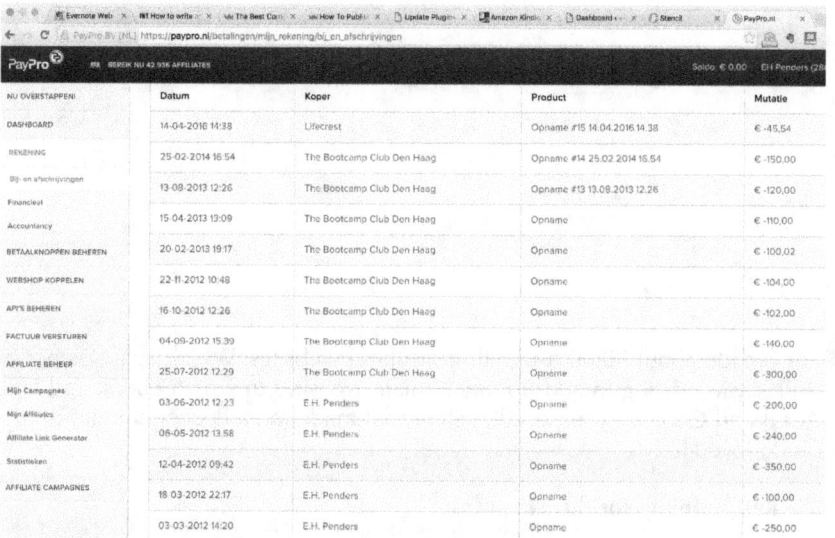

So thanks for reading this, it made me 45,00!

In 2012 I used my bootcamp business as the name, because it was easier with tax and stuff. This is over 2 years, but only because I had limited time and focus. It really wasn't that hard as you can read in this book. The most important thing I learned is something I already mentioned a few times.

You never know when you might be close to succeeding, this means if you choose to follow a certain strategy, keep going no matter what. Measure results and adjust as you go. But keep going. Only once you really feel you've proven it doesn't work, you should change strategies.

Conclusion

How and why these strategies have evolved

The strategies shown in this book still work, but are harder to execute at this time. It will probably continue to get harder in the future. I quickly want to share with you why and how these strategies have evolved and how I would use them right now (2016).

As you might know, Google updates now and then. Pinguin, Panda those kind of animals. (Google it if you have no clue what I'm talking about here) With these updates, Google tries to give the searching customer (you) the best experience. Which means, if you are looking for something, Google wants to provide you with answers.

Quality is one of the key factors for Google. And Google doesn't particularly see a lot of value in mini websites. Actually they devalue them. They believe these websites are optimized for rankings and not optimized for value to their users. That's why overly optimized mini websites are doomed nowadays. The only way to succeed is delivering exactly what searchers are looking for and provide value.

If you do that, Google will sent you traffic. (Although highly competitive markets are hard to get traffic on). It is smart however to optimize content for SEO, at least in a way you let Google know what your content is about. So your keyword(s) should be in the title, the url, headlines and in the copy.

Back in the old days you could just stuff your content with keywords and you would rank on the keyword. Those days are gone for good. Google's bots are getting more sophisticated (seemingly everyday) and they pick up on people that try to beat the system.

"Does this mean it's not possible to use these strategies right now?"

No, you need to use these strategies differently. Let me show you how…

My advice on how to use these strategies now

You have two options that will work best when you want to use these strategies. You can either;

1. **Create mini websites that are not as 'mini.' With more content, more backlinks, more value. And do this in lower competitive markets. How much content you need is hard to say. It depends on the niche you're in and the competition you're facing. Also how good your content is, if you have backlinks and the quality of these backlinks and if you've optimized for SEO.**

2. **Or create one 'big' website, also called an 'authority website'. Which takes longer to build, but will add up over time. If you do this in a niche market and create tons of valuable content optimized for SEO, you will be a happy camper later.**

"I would personally recommend to go for an 'authority website' about something you really like."

With an authority website you do things slightly different. You start by choosing one niche market. It should have acceptable competition levels and high enough search volumes. Than you create as many small sub topics that all relate to your main topic and you create a lot of valuable content on these topics.

Use market samurai and google's keyword tool to do some research and to create a content sheet in excel. Let me give you a quick example.

"These two tools are the only crucial tools you need."

Let's say you want to create a blog about coffee. You can line up your main topics about coffee using the keyword tool. If you enter coffee in the keyword tool like this;

🔍 Find new keywords and get search volume data

▾ Search for new keywords using a phrase, website or category

Enter one or more of the following:
Your product or service

coffee

Your landing page

www.example.com/page

Your product category

Enter or select a product category

Targeting ?

All locations

English

Google

Negative keywords

Date range ?

Show avg. monthly searches
for: last 12 months

Customize your search ?

Keyword filters

Keyword options
Show broadly related ideas
Hide keywords in my account
Hide keywords in my plan

Keywords to include

Get ideas

Click the 'get idea's button and you'll see something like this;

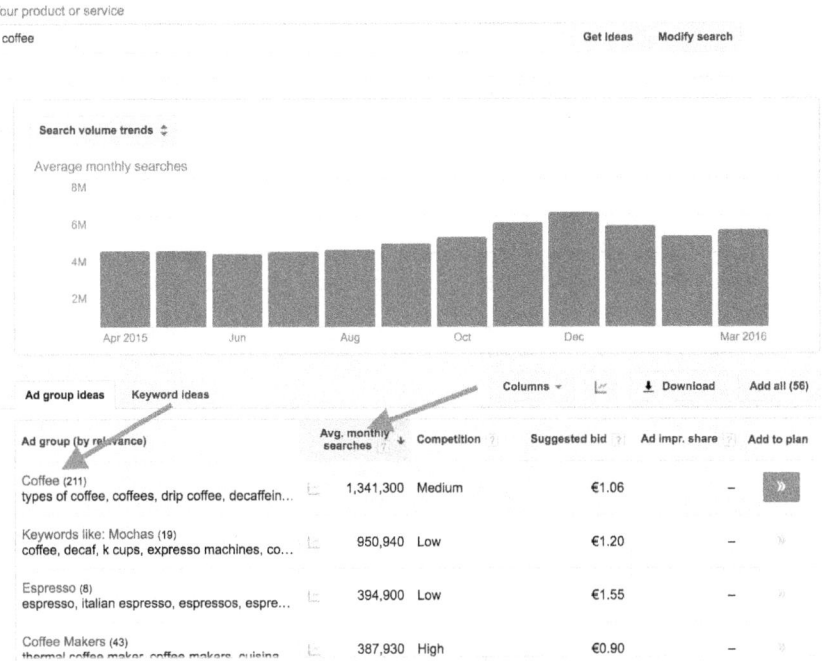

Click on the 'avg. Monthly searches' to get the highest search volume at the top. And click on the first one. (You can check them all out if you want, but for this example we use the first one) You'll see something like this;

Ad group: **Coffee**

1 of 56 ad group ideas   <   >

⬑

⬇ Download   Add all (211)

Keyword (by relevance)		Avg. monthly searches ↓	Competition	Suggested bid	Ad Impr. share	Add to plan
irish coffee	⬕	110,000	Low	€0.62	–	»
caribou coffee	⬕	110,000	Low	€2.01	–	»
coffee break	⬕	90,500	Low	€0.63	–	»
black coffee	⬕	60,500	Low	€0.29	–	»
coffee cake recipe	⬕	40,500	Low	€1.55	–	**»**
coffee cake	⬕	40,500	Low	€0.40	–	»
how to make coffee	⬕	40,500	Low	€1.45	–	»
caffeine in coffee	⬕	40,500	Low	€3.00	–	»

Click on the 'avg. Monthly searches' again, to get the highest volume to the top. As you can see you already have a few main topics you can choose to write about. I would put your 'main' topics in an excel sheet and create 'sub topics' as you go. So for this example that would look something like this;

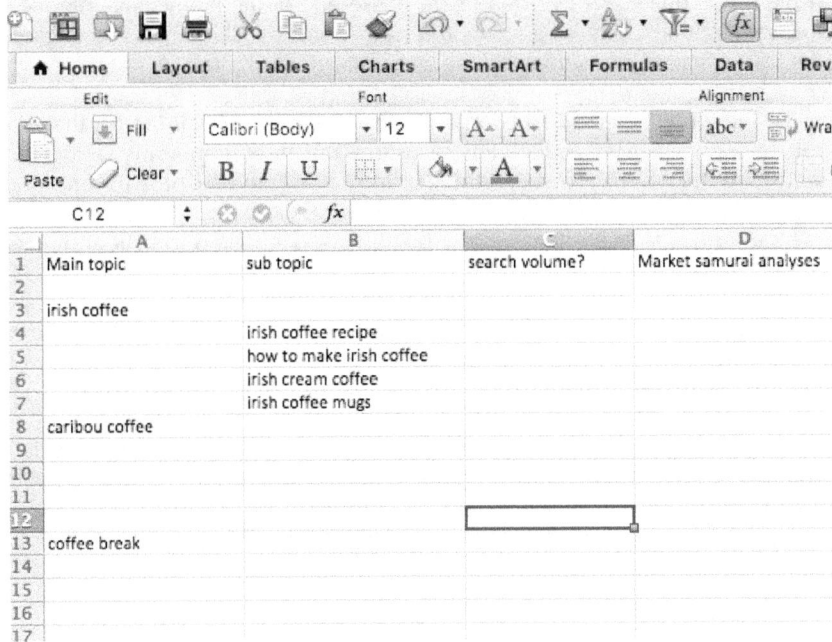

I like to add search volumes and the analyses I got from Market Samurai. Here is an example of a keyword in market samurai. I wanted to check out SEO competition on this keyword. Here you see the top rankers on this keyword;

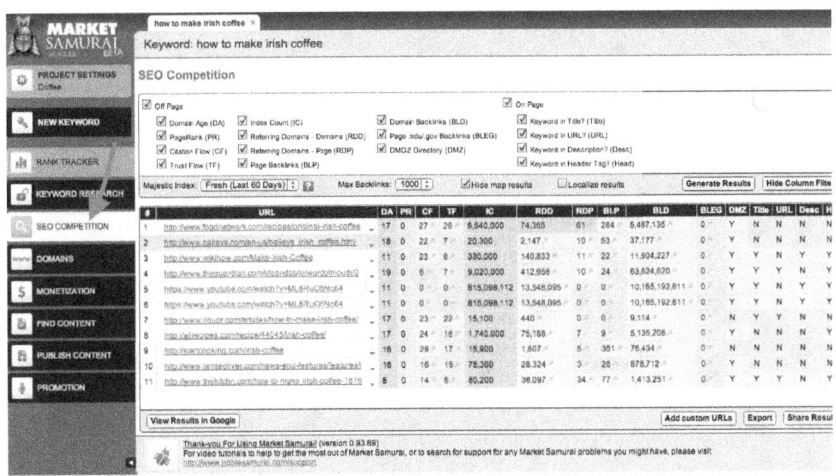

If you don't know Market Samurai this might seem like abracadabra. Let me explain real quick. All I've done here is use one of the many available tools of market samurai. I entered a keyword; 'how to make irish coffee' and clicked on the SEO competition button and the 'generate results' button.

At the top you see all sorts of fancy names, which are all factors that play a role in ranking. Market Samurai measures the most important factors of all websites. The colors you see is the first indicator how hard it is to rank on this keywords. The more red you see, the better that factor is with the competitor and the harder it is to beat them. Yellow is still reasonably hard to beat and green is pretty doable.

I can't go in to detail on how to use this tool, but this is information you want to get a hold of when you try to rank for certain keywords. There are many other tools in market samurai that are all very powerful. You get the point.

Streamlining and organizing your content plan is very important. Especially if you're a scatterbrain like me. So think about what you want to blog on. What's your passion? What would you like to share with the world or write about? If you can learn and create content, you can build a business.

Closing word

We're closing in on the end of this book. I had a lot of pleasure writing this for you, as it a personal story of excitement, frustration, and personal success. This is what truly showed me the opportunities online. This is what made me go back in the beginning of 2016. I am pursuing a new online dream right now as you are reading this. Care to join me?

Listen I say that with all sincerity. We can all succeed and I really want to help anyone that wants to do the work required. It will create tremendous rewards down the road. Freedom, prosperity and making a difference. No matter what topic you might want to create a business on.

Right now I'm not making a lot of money online, but it will come. I will continue to provide value for anyone that's willing to listen and in the end, that's what matters.

If this book was in any way valuable for you, I could really use a favor. Please go to Amazon and write me a review on this book. It takes two seconds and it really helps me sustain the work I do. Very much appreciated! Thank so much for your support and if you need my help or have questions, never hesitate to reach out to me on erikpenders.com or find me on Facebook.

I'm there many hours a day.

If there's one thing that really important in my journey, it's choosing one strategy and focusing solely on it. Go for one thing. Don't try to do everything, it will burn you out. This is still very important for me as I am building a new business from scratch.

Anyway, I want to thank you again for taking the time to read this and hope you will remain a dreamer and think of better days and more rewarding and fulfilling ways to spend your life.

Big hug,

Erik.

Other books I wrote

Starting an online business fast

This is the first book I wrote in this series;

You can get it here;

https://www.amazon.com/dp/B01BMAXH3S

www.ingramcontent.com/pod-product-compliance
Lightning Source LLC
Chambersburg PA
CBHW070416190526
45169CB00003B/1286